Polka Dot Girls

Designed. Original. Treasured.

By
Kristie Kerr & Paula Yarnes

Copyright 2011 Kristie Kerr and Paula Yarnes. All Rights Reserved.

No part of this book may be reproduced, transmitted, or utilized in any form or by any means,graphic, electronic or mechanical, including photocopying, recording, taping, or by any information storage or retrieval, without the permission in writing from the publisher. WITH THE EXCEPTION OF THE POLKA DOT PLUS WEEKLY CHALLENGES, TAKE HOME ACTIVITY SHEETS AND PARENT PARTNERS, WHICH MAY BE DUPLICATED FOR GROUP USE ONLY.

Unless otherwise indicated, all Scripture quotations are taken from the Holy Bible, New Living Translation, copyright © 1996, 2004, 2007 by Tyndale House Foundation. Used by permission of Tyndale House Publishers, Inc., Carol Stream, Illinois 60188. All rights reserved.

THE HOLY BIBLE, NEW INTERNATIONAL VERSION®, NIV® Copyright © 1973, 1978, 1984, 2011 by Biblica, Inc.™ Used by permission. All rights reserved worldwide.

Scripture taken from The Message. Copyright © 1993, 1994, 1995, 1996, 2000, 2001, 2002. Used by permission of NavPress Publishing Group.

Scripture taken from the Contemporary English Version © 1991, 1992, 1995 by American Bible Society, Used by Permission.

Scripture taken from the Common English Bible P.O. Box 801 201 Eighth Avenue South Nashville, TN 37202-0801

ISBN: 987-0-9840312-0-7

Printed in the United States of America

1st Printing

Contents

How To Use This Book 1

Getting to Know Him 3-26
Large Group Lesson 3
Polk Dot Talk
    Kindergarten – 1st Grade 11
    2nd – 3rd Grade 13
    4th – 5th Grade 15
Polka Dot Project 17
Polka Dot Plus
    Weekly Challenge 19
    Parent Partner 20
    Take Home Activity Sheets
        Kindergarten – 1st Grade 21
        2nd – 3rd Grade 23
        4th – 5th Grade 25

God the Father 27-52
Large Group Lesson 27
Polk Dot Talk
    Kindergarten – 1st Grade 35
    2nd – 3rd Grade 37
    4th – 5th Grade 39
Polka Dot Project 43
Polka Dot Plus
    Weekly Challenge 45
    Parent Partner 46
    Take Home Activity Sheets
        Kindergarten – 1st Grade 47
        2nd – 3rd Grade 49
        4th – 5th Grade 51

God the Son 53-74
Large Group Lesson 53
Polk Dot Talk
    Kindergarten – 1st Grade 59
    2nd – 3rd Grade 61
    4th – 5th Grade 63

Polka Dot Project 65
Polka Dot Plus
    Weekly Challenge 67
    Parent Partner 68
    Take Home Activity Sheets
        Kindergarten – 1st Grade 69
        2nd – 3rd Grade 71
        4th – 5th Grade 73

God the Holy Spirit 74-96
Large Group Lesson 74
Polk Dot Talk
    Kindergarten – 1st Grade 81
    2nd – 3rd Grade 83
    4th – 5th Grade 85
Polka Dot Project 87
Polka Dot Plus
    Weekly Challenge 89
    Parent Partner 90
    Take Home Activity Sheets
        Kindergarten – 1st Grade 91
        2nd – 3rd Grade 93
        4th – 5th Grade 95

Polka Dot Party 97

Dedicated to the girls who inspire us:

Anja who does funny accents...

JoJo who DEFIES ALL ODDS...

Catelyn who is a SURVIVOR...

Lucy who LOVES unconditionally...

Betty who LIGHTS UP THE ROOM...

Dottie who loves tutus AND FISHING POLES...

Meg who is so funny she could possibly be the next Lucille Ball...

Ling who is NOT AFRAID to speak her mind...

Natalie who can organize like nobody's business...

Jeorgia who has AMAZING COURAGE...

and Lily who is simply sweet!

You amaze us.
Go change the world.

How to Use this Book

It seems easy enough, right? Like you really shouldn't need a page just to tell you how to use this book. And yet, here we are. We are nothing if we're not efficient!

Ok. This resource was written as a tool for use in a large group, small group or even for your family to use. Obviously, your specific needs may vary according to the size and make up of your group, but we have hopefully provided you with enough options that you have plenty of... well, options.

Each chapter starts with a large group lesson. This is something that can be taught by one teacher or even a variety of leaders. These lessons are designed to appeal to all age groups – so bring all your girls together for this part of the session. There are stories and illustrations provided, but feel free to add in your own thoughts, insights and stories! The girls will love to hear about your own personal experiences and perspective.

Following the large group time, there are questions for small group discussion. These are broken down by grade level (K-1, 2-3, and 4-5)– so this would be a great time to divide the girls into smaller groups with separate leaders so that the discussion can be tailored to fit their level of experience and understanding. (If you don't have enough leaders to do small groups, keep the girls together and alternate questions from the various age level discussion questions.) Close out your small group time with a time of prayer. Invite the girls to pray for each other and take turns praying out loud. Not only will you learn a lot about your girls during this time, their little hearts will be bonded together when they spend time praying for one another.

Then it's craft time! We've included lots of fun ideas for you to do as a group. Make sure you do adequate preparation depending on the age and skill level of your girl. Nothing is more frustrating than running out of time because you spent too much time cutting things out or waiting for glue to dry. (By the way... glue dries REALLY slow. Even slower when you want it to dry fast. Just our experience anyway....)

Lastly, we've included some pages to be photocopied and sent home. They include a weekly challenge for the girls, age appropriate activity sheets, and a parent partner. These are intended to give the girls some fun tools to work on throughout the week and to let the parents keep up with what their daughters are learning.

And the MOST important thing to remember is to MAKE IT WORK FOR YOU. Every group is unique and different, so feel free to add, subtract, edit, rewrite, and rework anything you find here. Find out what works and stick with it and don't be afraid to chuck the stuff that isn't working.

Our job is simple – but it couldn't be more important. We get the amazing privilege of teaching these sweet girls about Jesus. We pray the material gives you practical tools to do just that. But above and beyond all that, remember that your gift of time and interest in these girls' lives will impact them far greater than any lesson or illustration. You are literally demonstrating for them what it means to be a woman who loves Jesus. Be patient. Be loving. Be fun. Be there.

We wish you all the best as you teach your girls what it means to be a Polka Dot girl!

Knowing God

week 1

Getting to Know Him

WHAT'S THE POINT?
GOD KNOWS EVERYTHING ABOUT YOU,
AND HE WANTS YOU TO KNOW EVERYTHING ABOUT HIM.

theme verse
The Lord is close to all who call on Him.
Psalm 145:18

related bible story
Exodus 4:1-17

❋ Large Group Lesson ❋

Do you have a best friend? What is her name? How do you know her? Why is she your friend?

Have you ever met somebody and thought to yourself right away, "I want to be her friend?" You look at her and she seems so nice or fun or smart and you just want to know more about her?

I had a friend once named Sarah. I met her at school, and she made me laugh. She was very nice to people and wore pretty shoes. I knew right away that I wanted to be Sarah's friend. So, I started talking to her. I asked her about the things that she liked. The amazing thing was that she liked the same things I liked!

She liked chocolate ice cream cones and puppies and playing school and hated wearing dresses. Just like me! And the more time I spent with Sarah, the more I learned about her… and the more I liked her. She was a very good friend.

And you know what? It's the same way with God. Sometimes it can seem like God is great big and far away. It can feel like He is just way to big to care about something as little as me. But the truth is, God wants to be your friend!

Isn't that crazy! The great big God who made all the stars and oceans and makes the snow fall from heaven wants to be friends with YOU!

O Lord, You are the friend of your worshippers… – Psalm 25:10 (CEV)

God already knows EVERYTHING about you. He knows what you're thinking, what you're feeling, what you are going to do today, and even what you are going to do tomorrow! The Bible tells us that He even knows how many hairs you have on your head!

> I Peter 1:2 says, *God the Father knew you and chose you long ago.* Not only does He know everything about you, but He CHOSE you to be His friend! Imagine the coolest, smartest, most amazing person in the universe deciding that out of all the people in the entire world – they wanted to be friends with you. That's pretty amazing to me!

God knows you. God loves you. And God wants you to know Him too.

So, how do you get to know God better? The same way I got to know my friend Sarah. By discovering what He is like. By spending time together. By learning about the things that are important to Him. By finding out what He cares about.

God knows everything about you, and He wants you to know everything about Him.

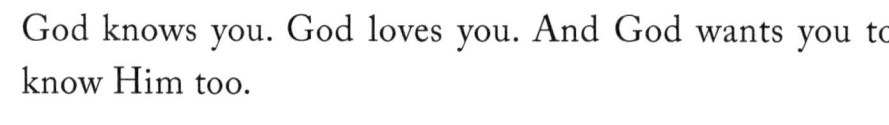

Polka Dot Girls ❀ Knowing God

week 1

There are 3 ways we can get to know God better!

➡ 1. Reading The Bible

The Bible is a letter from God to you! God had LOTS of things that He wanted to say to you. He wanted to tell you about Himself. He wanted to tell you about things He had done for other people. He wanted to give you instructions on how you could live your life in a way that would make Him happy.

I have hidden your word in my heart, that I might not sin against you. – Psalm 119:11 NLT

So, He gave us the Bible. He told some people many, many years ago to write down some very special stories and words that would help you and me be able to understand Him better. And now, you and I can read the Bible and learn what God is like!

You can read the stories and see how God helped people. You can see how He told them to live. You can learn about His heart and how He thinks and most importantly how very, very much He loves you.

My friend Emily was facing something difficult and she didn't know what to do. She had to get up in front of her whole class and give a book report. Emily was *Scared to Death* of talking in front of people. Her knees would shake and her hands would get sweaty and her tummy wouldn't feel so good. What was she going to do?

She opened her Bible one day, and found a story about a man named Moses. God asked Moses to lead His people out of a really bad situation. He was to go before the Pharoah, who was the King of Egypt and tell him to let God's people go. Moses was SCARED! He did not want to stand in front of the King. I can imagine that his knees would shake and his hands would get sweaty and his tummy wouldn't feel so good… just like Emily.

But, here is what God said to Moses. *When you speak, I will be with you and give you the words to say.* – Exodus 4:12 CEV

WHOA! That is exactly what Emily needed to hear. It was so cool to see that the words that God had said to Moses in the Bible could be so helpful to Emily. She wrote the words on a little card and carried it with her the days before she had to give her speech. When the day finally came, she read the card one more time, took a deep breath, and got up in front of the class confident that God was with her and that He would help her do her very best.

The Bible is FULL of stories just like this one that can help us get through the things we face in our lives. It has all kinds of wisdom and special help for us. There are so many times when I open up my Bible and find a verse that totally encourages me.

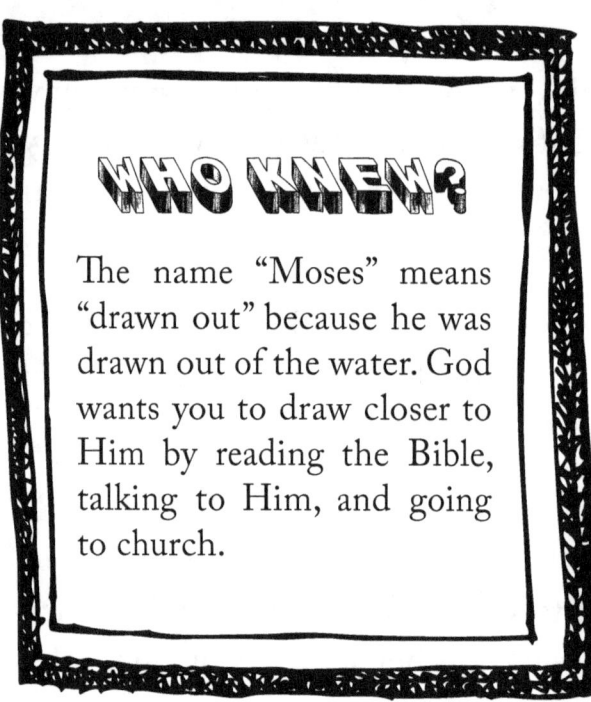

WHO KNEW?

The name "Moses" means "drawn out" because he was drawn out of the water. God wants you to draw closer to Him by reading the Bible, talking to Him, and going to church.

God uses the Bible to speak to us, but it also tells us what God is like. We learn that He is faithful. Hosea 2:20 says, *I will be faithful to you and make you mine.* We can know, by reading the Bible, that God will never let us down.

We learn that God is perfect. He never makes mistakes. He never changes. We can know that He will love us the same today as He did yesterday and will love us just as much tomorrow.

The Bible is God's letter to you. It's important that you read it everyday so that you can learn more and more what God is like. That is how you get closer to him!

Polka Dot Girls ❧ Knowing God

week 1

The second way we can know God better is:

➡ 2. By Talking to God

Have you ever had a really long talk with a good friend? Maybe you have had a sleepover at your house with your best friend and you have laid in bed talking about what you want to be when you grow up, or your favorite movie or maybe even what you're afraid of.

I don't know about you, but when I talk to my friends something really cool happens between us. I feel closer to that person. I feel better about the things I'm going through. I know that I'm not alone and that there is someone who wants to hear the things that I care about.

And God wants us to talk to Him just like we talk to one of our friends. Actually, "praying" to God is really just talking to God! He wants you to come to Him with the things that are bothering you. He wants you to tell Him the things you are excited about and what you are thankful for. He loves it when you share your heart with Him.

And something will happen to your heart when you tell God your thoughts, worries, and problems. You will begin to feel closer to Him just like you do when you are talking to your friends! It's so nice to know that He cares about the things that you care about. He is *Always* listening – and is the best friend you could ever want to have!

And not only can you talk to God, but God will talk to you!

Ask me, and I will tell you remarkable secrets… – Jeremiah 33:3 NLT

You may not hear His voice out loud like you hear your Mom or Dad, but God whispers to your heart. When God speaks to me, it's like I hear words in my head that I know weren't my own idea. I always try to write down the words that I feel God is speaking to my heart so that I can remember what He is saying to me. And the amazing thing is that when God speaks to you, it will ALWAYS line up with what the Bible says! So, whenever I hear Him speak, I go to my Bible and find verses that confirm what He has said to my heart.

God will give you answers to your problems. He will challenge you to do better with your attitude or behavior. He will make you feel better when you're sad or upset. He will talk to you about your future. If you will listen, God will speak to you.

One of my **ALL TIME** favorite verses in the Bible is Psalm 27:8. It says, *My heart has heard you say, "Come and talk with me.* And my heart responds, 'Lord, I am coming.' This verse makes me imagine God, calling my name and saying, "Hey Kristie… come on over here and sit down and tell me about your day. What's going on? How are you doing?" I imagine myself sitting right next to God just talking to Him about everything. It makes me feel so close to Him when we have those times together.

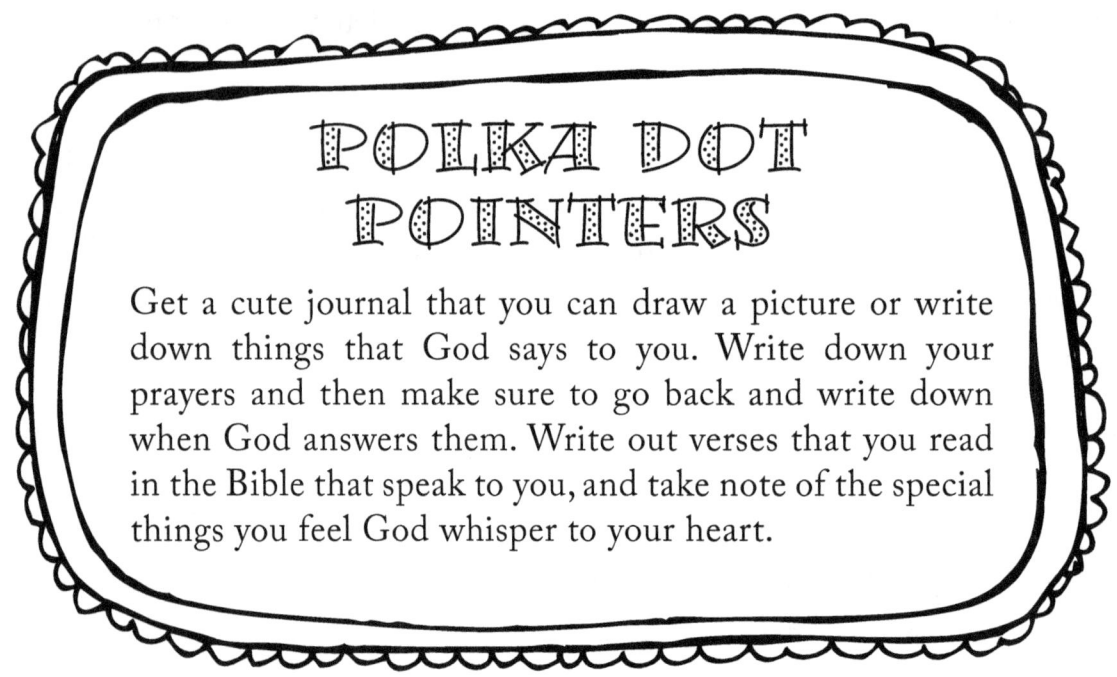

POLKA DOT POINTERS

Get a cute journal that you can draw a picture or write down things that God says to you. Write down your prayers and then make sure to go back and write down when God answers them. Write out verses that you read in the Bible that speak to you, and take note of the special things you feel God whisper to your heart.

And the last way we can grow closer to God is to:

➡ 3. Go to church.

Every morning, you wake up, comb your hair, brush your teeth, put on your clothes and do what? GO TO SCHOOL! How many of you like school?!

Why do you go to school every day? To learn! You go to school so that you can learn about reading and science and math. There are teachers there that show you how

week 1

to do things. You can discover all kinds of new ideas by listening to your teachers.

Church is a place where you can learn more about God! You will hear stories about the things He has done in the past. You will learn about the things in the Bible. You will learn the things that make God happy and the things that He doesn't want you to do. (You will make lots of great friends and have a lot of fun too!!)

It's important that you read your Bible and talk to God when you are at home. But there is something really amazing that happens when you come together with other people who believe in God like you do and learn about Him. It helps you grow stronger in your faith. You can talk to your teachers and your Christian friends about God. You can ask questions about the things you are unsure about. You can have people pray for you and your family.

Make sure that you come to church regularly! It's important to spend time with other people who believe in God like you do!

Summary: You can know God. You can learn about Him. You can talk to Him. He wants to be your very best friend.

God knows everything about you, and He wants you to know everything about Him.

Closing Prayer: *Dear God, thank you that you know me. Thank you that you want to be my very best friend. I want to know more and more about you too. Help me to spend time reading the Bible, talking to you, and learning more about you at church. Thank you for choosing me to be your friend. Amen.*

ILLUSTRATION: Have something heavy on the stage, like a big rock. Have one girl come up and try and lift it by herself. It will be too heavy for her to carry on her own. Then have a few other girls help her lift the object.

CONCLUSION: Sometimes we need others to help us. We can't do it on our own and we need the help of our friends to support us, help us, and pray for us.

Polka Dot Girls ❦ Knowing God

week 1

Kindergarten and 1st Grade Group Discussion Questions

1. How do you get to know your friends?

    a. By playing with them.

    b. By talking to them.

    c. By spending time with them.

    d. By learning about the things they like to do.

2. God wants to be your friend! He wants you to know everything about Him. What were the three ways we can grow closer to God that we talked about during the lesson?

    a. Reading the Bible.

    b. Talking to God.

    c. Going to Church.

3. Why is it important that we read the Bible? What can we learn about God through reading His letter to us?

    a. We learn more about God.

    b. We learn what He is like.

    c. We can know the way He wants us to live our lives.

4. Do you talk to God? What have you talked to God about?

    a. Prayed for a sick friend.

    b. Thanked Him for our food before we eat.

    c. Saying prayers before we go to sleep.

    b. Although it's really nice to say your prayers with your mom or dad, you can talk to God all by yourself!

5. Have you ever felt like God talked back to you? What did He say?

    a. We prayed for a sick friend and she got better.

    b. I asked God to help me not be afraid, and now I'm not anymore!

6. What have you learned about God by coming to church?

    a. I've learned that God loves me.

    b. I've learned that God is my friend.

    c. I've learned that God wants to help me.

7. Practice saying our theme verse together a few times.

The Lord is close to all who call on Him.
– Psalm 145:18

week 1

2nd and 3rd Grade Group Discussion Questions

1. How do you get to know your friends?

    a. By playing with them.

    b. By talking to them.

    c. By spending time with them.

    d. By learning about the things they like to do.

2. God wants to be your friend! He wants you to know everything about Him. What were the three ways we can grow closer to God that we talked about during the lesson?

    a. Reading the Bible.

    b. Talking to God.

    c. Going to Church.

3. Why is it important that we read the Bible? What can we learn about God through reading His letter to us?

    a. We learn more about God.

    b. We learn what He is like.

    c. We can know the way He wants us to live our lives.

    d. We can learn right from wrong.

4. Do you talk to God? What have you talked to God about?

    a. Prayed for a sick friend.

    b. Thanked Him for our food before we eat.

    c. Saying prayers before we go to sleep.

    d. Prayed about something that was bothering you

5. Have you ever felt like God talked back to you?
  What did He say?

    a. We prayed for a sick friend and she got better.

    b. I asked God to help me not be afraid, and now I'm not anymore!

    c. God helped you work through a tough situation

6. What have you learned about God by coming to church?

    a. I've learned that God loves me.

    b. I've learned that God is my friend.

    c. I've learned that God wants to help me.

    d. I've learned that God never changes and I can always count on Him.

7. Practice saying our theme verse together a few times.

The Lord is close to all who call on Him.
Psalm 145:18

Polka Dot Girls ♣ Knowing God

week 1

4th and 5th Grade
Group Discussion Questions

1. Do you think there is a difference between **KNOWING ABOUT** someone and actually **KNOWING** them?

    a. Tell me 5 things you know about _____.

    (Teachers – put in the name of a celebrity that would be appropriate and someone your girls would know – like Justin Bieber, Hannah Montana, etc.)

    b. So you know a lot **ABOUT** them – but do you really **KNOW** them?

    c. What is the difference between knowing someone and knowing about them?

        i. You actually talk to the people you know.
        ii. You spend time with them.
        iii. You don't pick up the phone and call a celebrity... but you can find out the facts about them.

    d. God doesn't want you to just know **ABOUT** Him, He wants you to actually **KNOW** Him!

        i. So make sure you don't just learn the facts about God, but that you really spend time talking with Him and getting to know Him.

2. What were the three ways we can grow closer to God that we talked about during the lesson?

    a. Reading the Bible
    b. Talking to God
    c. Going to Church

3. Why is it important that we read the Bible? What can we learn about God through reading His letter to us?

    a. We learn more about God.
    b. We learn what He is like.
    c. We can know the way He wants us to live our lives.
    d. We can learn right from wrong.

    e. We can understand His character.

4. Do you talk to God? What have you talked to God about?
    a. Prayed for a sick friend.
    b. Thanked Him for our food before we eat.
    c. Saying prayers before we go to sleep.
    d. Prayed about something that was bothering you.

5. Have you ever felt like God talked back to you? What did He say?
    a. We prayed for a sick friend and she got better.
    b. I asked God to help me not be afraid, and now I'm not anymore!
    c. God helped you work through a tough situation.
    d. I read my Bible and God showed me a verse that really helped me.

6. What have you learned about God by coming to church?
    a. I've learned that God loves me.
    b. I've learned that God is my friend.
    c. I've learned that God wants to help me.
    d. I've learned that God never changes and I can always count on Him.

7. Practice saying our theme verse together a few times.
    The Lord is close to all who call on Him.
    – Psalm 145:18

week 1

"I Know God" Book

Leaders: Make sure you do adequate preparation for the crafts in accordance to the age and skill level of your group. For younger children, have the key words already cut out or even printed on peel and stick address labels. Older children should be able to cut out and glue in the allotted time.

Supplies Needed:

- Copies of the key words (provided)
- Bibles (to look up verses)
- 3 sheets of 8 x 11 pretty paper per Polka Dot girl:
  Cut the three sheets in half, each girl will receive 6 sheets of paper. One for the cover and five for the pages of the book.
- Glue
- Scissors
- Stapler
- Markers
- Stickers, embellishments, glitter, etc.

Prep:

1. Put together the six sheets of pretty paper.
2. Staple the pretty paper three times on the left side to make a book.
3. Make copies of the key words (provided) for each Polka Dot girl.

What should we do?

1. Give each girl a book of pretty paper.
2. Have each girl cut out the key words that were pre-printed.
3. Glue a keyword on each page.
4. Decorate each page with pretty stickers and embellishments.

Keywords:

God is **LOVE**

1 John 4:8 – *But anyone who does not love does not know God, for **God is love**.*

God is **KIND**

Psalm 116:5 – *How **kind** the Lord is! How good he is! So merciful, this God of ours!*

God **KNOWS EVERYTHING**

Psalm 139:1 – *O Lord, you have examined my heart and **know everything** about me.*

God **NEVER CHANGES**

Hebrews 13:8 – *Jesus Christ **is the same** yesterday, today, and forever.*

God is **PATIENT**

Romans 2:4 – *Don't you see how wonderfully kind, tolerant, and **patient** God is with you?*

Polka Dot Girls ❧ Knowing God

Polka Dot Plus

week 1

Weekly Challenge

Grow – GROW your faith by reading the following Bible Story: **Exodus 4:1-17**

Love – Show God's LOVE this week by making a card for a friend or family member.

Act – Take ACTION: Do ONE thing to help you know God better. Talk to God about something you're worried or excited about. Go to church. Next week, share with your group what you did!

Memorize – MEMORIZE the theme verse for this week.

The Lord is close to all who call on Him.
– Psalm 145:18

Parent Partner

This week we:

- 🌀 Talked about knowing God.

- 🌀 Discussed the fact that God knows everything about us, and He wants us to know everything about Him. We can be close to Him and come to Him with everything we are facing.

- 🌀 Challenged the girls to grow closer to God by reading the Bible, talking to God, and going to church.

You can reinforce these ideas with your daughter by helping them grown in these three areas. Take time to pray with your daughter before bed. And let them take a turn saying the prayer! Have them connect with things that they did that day and thank God for them. Also have them remember the things they struggled with or were fearful of and ask God to help them with those things as well. It's important for them to learn to come to God with everything they are going through – and to turn to Him.

You can also help them look up verses in the Bible. Maybe they are struggling with fear. Get a good concordance or even look online for verses that will help them with. Write them out and help your daughter remember the promises God has given them when they are feeling fearful.

Lastly, be faithful in bringing your daughter to Polka Dot Girls and other church services and events. I know that the amount of activities that our kids are in these days can be overwhelming and sometimes the LAST thing you want to do is drive them one more place. But it is SO important for them to learn to prioritize spending time learning about God and being around people who can help build up their faith. We are living in critical days, and the more we can equip our children with the knowledge of who God is, the better. You will be sending them out into the world with a toolbox FULL of lessons and preparation to live a life pleasing to the Lord.

week 1

Kindergarten and 1st Grade Take Home Activity Sheet

In the space provided, draw a picture of you and your closest friend.

God wants to be your very best friend! The verses below talk about knowing God. Read each verse and write the word KNOW in the blank spaces. All scripture NIV.

Psalm 9:10 – *Those who _____ your name trust in you.*

Psalm 119:168 – *Yes, I obey your commandments and laws because you _____ everything I do.*

Psalm 139:23 – *Search me, O God, and _____ my heart.*

Daniel 11:32 – *But the people who _____ their God will be strong and will resist him.*

Phil 3:10 – *I want to _____ Christ and experience the mighty power that raised him from the dead.*

Col 1:10 – *You will grow as you learn to _____ God better and better.*

Polka Dot Girls ❖ Knowing God

week 1

2nd and 3rd Grade
Take Home Activity Sheet

In the space provided, draw a picture of you and your closest friend.

God wants to be your closest friend! He knows everything about you, and wants you to know everything about Him.

The verses below talk about knowing God. Look up each verse in your Bible and find the common word. Fill in the blank. All scripture NIV.

Psalm 9:10 – *Those who _____ your name trust in you, for you, O lord, do not abandon those who search for you.*

Psalm 119:168 – *Yes, I obey your commandments and laws because you _____ everything I do.*

Psalm 139:23 – *Search me, O God, and _____ my heart.*

Daniel 11:32 – *But the people who _____ their God will be strong and will resist him.*

John 10:27 – *My sheep listen to my voice; I _____ them, and they follow me.*

Phil 3:8 – *Yes, everything else is worthless when compared with the infinite value of _____ ing Christ Jesus my Lord. For his sake, I have discarded everything else, counting it all as garbage, so that I could gain Christ and become one with him.*

Phil 3:10 – *I want to _____ Christ and experience the mighty power that raised him from the dead.*

Col 1:10 – *All the while, you will grow as you learn to _____ God better and better.*

Polka Dot Girls ❀ Knowing God

week 1

4th and 5th Grade

God knows everything about you, and wants you to know everything about Him. The verses below talk about knowing God.

Look up each verse in your Bible and find the common word. Fill in the blank. All scripture NIV.

Psalm 9:10 – *Those who _____ your name _____ in you, for you, O lord, do not abandon those who search for you.*

Psalm 119:168 – *Yes, I obey your commandments and laws because you _____ everything I do.*

Psalm 139:23 – *Search me, O God, and _____ my _____.*

Daniel 11:32 – *But the people who _____ their God will be _____ and will resist him.*

John 10:27 – *My sheep listen to my voice; I _____ them, and they _____ me.*

Phil 3:8 – *Yes, everything else is _____ when compared with the infinite value of _____ Christ Jesus my Lord. For his sake, I have discarded everything else, counting it all as garbage, so that I could gain Christ and become one with him.*

Phil 3:10 – *I want to _____ Christ and experience the mighty _____ that raised him from the dead.*

Col 1:10 – *All the while, you will _____ as you learn to _____ God better and better.*

Polka Dot Girls ❖ Knowing God

Knowing God
week 2

God the Father

WHAT'S THE POINT?

GOD IS OUR HEAVENLY FATHER.
HE LOVES US,
PROTECTS US,
AND PROVIDES FOR US.

theme verse

*See how much our Father loves us,
for he calls us his children, and that is what we are!*
1 John 3:1

related bible story

Exodus 16:1-31

❊ **Large Group Lesson** ❊

Last week we talked about the fact that God knows everything about you – and that He wants you to know everything about Him. We talked about how we can learn more about God.

Who remembers the three ways we can grow closer to God?

➡ 1. Read the Bible

➡ 2. Talk to God

➡ 3. Go to church

Today we're going to talk some more about what God is like.

One of the most amazing things about God is that there are three different parts to who God is. Let me show you what I mean.

Trinity illustration:

Objective: to teach the concept of the Trinity. God known to us in three persons – God the Father, God the Son (Jesus) and God the Holy Spirit. Although there are three different parts to him, they are all God.

Hold up pitcher of water.

What is this? (water)

This is a pitcher of water. You can drink it on a hot day. You can take a shower or bath and get cleaned up with water. You can put it on your flowers and it will help them grow.

What is this? (Ice cubes)

These are ice cubes. How do you make ice cubes? You put water in these trays, and then put it in the freezer and it gets really, really cold and then you have ice cubes!

What is this? (steam)

This is steam. I put water in a kettle (or a steamer would work too…) and then I turn the heat on and it gets really, really hot and then you have steam!

What do all three of these things have in common? They are ALL water. But they are ALL different. They are different FORMS of the same thing. Water – ice – and steam.

Polka Dot Girls ❀ Knowing God

week 2

God is the same way! There are three parts to Him. They are all different forms, but they are all the same thing. The same way we have water, ice and steam – we have God the Father, God the Son or Jesus and God the Holy Spirit. They are one, but different.

Over the next few weeks, we are going to talk about the three different parts of God – the Father, Son, and Holy Spirit. We're going to learn about each one of them and what makes them different and special.

So, today we're going to start by talking about God the Father.

I think it's really, really cool that God calls himself our "Father." Cause fathers are really, really special.

Amber loves to spend time with her Dad. They have a lot in common, especially when it comes to the outdoors. They both love to be outside, go camping, and ride their bikes. Every year, they take a trip to a special camping spot, just the two of them. They set up their tents, build their campfires and spend a whole week hiking, fishing, and spending time together.

Amber absolutely loves the time with her dad. She always knows that he is going to make sure she is safe. He watches over her and keeps her away from anything dangerous or scary. Sometimes at night, she will hear a strange noise and she will start to get scared. But as soon as she remembers that her Dad is there with her, she isn't scared anymore because she knows that he is there protecting her.

AND GOD THE FATHER IS THE SAME WAY WITH YOU AND ME.

⇨ 1. God is our PROTECTOR

He is always watching over us, protecting us and keeping us safe from danger and harm. Psalm 121:7-8 gives us a really cool picture of how God protects us. It says, *"The Lord keeps you from all harm and watches over your life. The Lord keeps watch over you as you come and go, both now and forever."*

God is always watching over you. In those moments when you feel afraid of something, you can be sure that God is right there with you, keeping you safe. You don't have to be scared or ever, ever, ever feel like you are alone. God is watching over you. He is our protector.

> **Object lesson:** Have someone come to the front and hold up a shield *(a garbage can lid, a toy shield, or anything else you can find. They can also wear knee pads, goggles, or anything else you can think of.)*
>
> Then have some other girls come up and either shoot Nerf guns, or throw soft balls or anything else you can think of at the girl who will be safe because the shield protects her.

What is a protector? Well, it's like a shield in front of us.

This shield was a protector! No matter what we threw at her, she was safe because her shield was in front of her – making sure that nothing could get to her.

God is YOUR shield! He stands before you and around you and keeps you safe. Psalm 27:1 says, *"The Lord is my light and my salvation – so why should I be afraid? The Lord is my fortress, protecting me from danger, so why should I tremble?"* You don't ever have to be afraid, because you can know that God is watching over you and will protect you from harm.

Polka Dot Girls ❀ Knowing God

Another great thing about Amber's trips with her dad is that He makes sure she has everything she needs. He packs the cooler with lots of yummy things for them to eat. He catches the fish that they cook over the fire and eat for dinner. He makes sure she has clothes that are warm enough and shoes that will keep her feet safe and dry. He bought her a new sleeping bag that is extra warm for the nights when it gets cold outside. Amber never has to worry, because she knows that her Dad will provide everything she needs.

And God the Father is the same way with you and me.

2. God is our PROVIDER

Everything you and I have, has been given to us by God the Father. I know it may seem like your mom or dad or grandma bought you all the things you need. But the Bible tells us that everything we have has come from Him. He provides a job for your mom and dad so they can earn money to buy you things. He makes sure that you have the things you need every single day.

There is a story in Exodus chapter 16 which tells us about God providing for His people. The Israelites had just escaped the land of Egypt and now were on a journey to a new place to live. They were in the desert and there was nothing to eat. They were so hungry and they wondered what they were going to do.

So they prayed to God, and he did something amazing. In the morning, when they got out of their tents and went outside, there was food covering the ground called "manna." Every morning, the manna would fall from heaven and the people would gather it and eat it. God provided food for them every single day!

God is your provider. He provides your food, clothes, toys, and games. He makes sure that you have all the things you need. Sometimes we can worry about things, but it's important to remember that God will always provide for you.

Matthew 6:25-27 says this: *That is why I tell you not to worry about everyday life – whether you have enough food and drink, or enough clothes to wear. Isn't life more than food, and your body more than clothing? Look at the birds. They don't plant or harvest or store food in barns, for your heavenly Father feeds them. And aren't you far more valuable to him that they are? Can all your worries add a single moment to your life?*

Did you catch that? God is even making sure that the birds you see outside in the trees have enough food and a place to live. And God cares WAY more for you than for the birds!! He will always make sure you are taken care of. That is His job as your Heavenly Father.

POLKA DOT POINTERS

Sometimes it's easy to forget that everything we have comes from God. To help you to remember that God has given you all the things in your life, try this. Every time you eat some food or get some new clothes or toys, stop and whisper "thank you" to Jesus. It will help you remember that all your blessings come from Him.

Our friend Amber loves her dad so much. He is a really, really good Dad. He spends time with her and helps her learn lots of things and he really, really loves her. But you know what? Sometimes her Dad makes mistakes. Sometimes He gets frustrated and says something that hurts her feelings. Sometimes he has to work a lot and cannot be there for her when she really needs someone to talk to. As much as Amber's dad loves her, he is still human, and he makes mistakes.

And that is why it is so important that we know God as our Heavenly Father. You know why?

Polka Dot Girls ❧ Knowing God

week 2

→ 3. Because God the Father is PERFECT

God is like our earthly Fathers in SO many ways, but there is one way that He is absolutely different. God the Father doesn't EVER make mistakes. He ALWAYS does the right thing and He ALWAYS does what is best for you.

See, no matter how much your Mom and Dad love you, they are still people just like you and me. And people make mistakes. How many of you here have ever made a mistake? How many of you have every said or done something that hurt another person's feelings? How many of you have ever done something that you wish you could take back? All of us have, because we are humans – and humans are NOT perfect.

But God is not human. He is God. He never, ever, ever makes a mistake. That makes me feel so SAFE! I can know that no matter what, God will love me perfectly, treat me perfectly, and do the absolute best thing for me every time. I don't ever have to wonder if God forgot about me or is mad at me or doesn't love me anymore. He will never ever let me down. He will never ever fail me. He will never ever do anything that isn't PERFECT.

JUST SO YOU KNOW:

Some girls don't have a dad in their life. There are lots of reasons that this may be the case. You should know that it is NEVER your fault if you don't have a dad who is close to you. It must be really hard sometimes to wish you had a dad like other girls. But you should know that God promises that He will be the very best Father you could ever imagine. There is even a verse in the Bible JUST for you. It says in Psalm 68:5, *A father to the fatherless, a defender of widows, is God in His holy dwelling*. You may not have a father here on earth, or maybe you do have a father but you are not close to him. God will step in and be the best father you ever dreamed of having. It's His promise to you.

God is your Heavenly Father. He loves you so much. You are His most precious daughter and He thinks you are amazing. Whenever you are scared, think of your Heavenly Father standing before you, protecting you and keeping you safe. When you're worried about something, remember that He is your Father who will give you everything you need. And when you need to know that you can count on someone to always be there for you, you can count on your perfect, unchanging Father God.

Closing Prayer: *God, thank you for being my Father. It makes me feel so special and safe to know that you are taking care of me. Help me to always remember that I am your daughter and that you love me. Amen.*

Polka Dot Girls ❧ Knowing God

week 2

Kindergarten and 1st Grade Group Discussion Questions

1. Tonight we learned about God and how there are three parts to Him. Do you remember what the three parts are?
   a. God the Father
   b. God the Son (Jesus)
   c. God the Holy Spirit

2. God the Father is our protector. What does the word "protector" mean?
   a. Someone that makes sure you are safe.
   b. The person that sticks up for you.
   c. Someone who fights for you.

3. How does is make you feel to know that God is watching over you?
   a. Safe
   b. Happy
   c. Peaceful
   d. Not afraid
   e. Confident

4. God the Father is our provider. What does the word "provider" mean?
   a. Someone who makes sure you have all the things you need
   b. The person that gives you food and clothes
   d. Someone that gives you money

5. There is a difference between something you need and something you want. Name a few things that are things you NEED.
   a. Food
   b. Clothes
   c. House to live in

6. Now name a few things that are WANTS.
   a. Toys
   b. Games
   c. Computers
   d. New bike

It's important to remember that God promises to provide the things that we need. That doesn't mean that we get everything we WANT. BUT – sometimes God blesses us by giving us the things we NEED and some of the things we want. That is why we should be so thankful for the things we have… because God gave them to us!

7. There is a really cool verse in the Bible about God being our provider. 2 Corinthians 9:8 says, *And God will generously provide all you need. You will always have everything you need and plenty left over to share with others.* What do you think this verse means?

   a. God will always give you what you need.
   b. God is generous with us… which means He gives us lots of super awesome things.
   c. God will give us things and we're supposed to share with others what God has given to us.

8. Practice saying the first part of this verse together a few times: *And God will generously provide all you need.* – 2 Corinthians 9:8

9. What does it mean to be "PERFECT?"
   a. Never make mistakes
   b. Always do the right thing
   c. Never say something wrong

10. Do you know anyone who is perfect?
    a. No! Only God is perfect. All of us make mistakes, but God NEVER does. God is perfect!

11. How does it make you feel to know that God is perfect and will never let you down?
    a. Safe
    b. Happy
    c. Comforted

Polka Dot Girls ❦ Knowing God

week 2

2nd and 3rd Grade Group Discussion Questions

1. Tonight we learned about God and how there are three parts to Him. Do you remember what the three parts are?
   a. God the Father
   b. God the Son (Jesus)
   c. God the Holy Spirit

2. God the Father is our protector. What does the word "protector" mean?
   a. Someone that makes sure you are safe.
   b. The person that sticks up for you.
   c. Someone who fights for you.

3. How does is make you feel to know that God is watching over you?
   a. Safe
   b. Happy
   c. Peaceful
   d. Not afraid
   e. Confident

4. God the Father is our provider. What does the word "provider" mean?
   a. Someone who makes sure you have all the things you need
   b. The person that gives you food and clothes
   c. Someone that gives you money

5. There is a difference between something you need and something you want. Name a few things that are things you NEED.
   a. Food
   b. Clothes
   c. House to live in

6. Now name a few things that are WANTS.
   a. Toys
   b. Games
   c. Computers
   d. New bike

It's important to remember that God promises to provide the things that we need. That doesn't mean that we get everything we WANT. BUT – sometimes God blesses us by giving us the things we NEED and some of the things we want. That is why we should be so thankful for the things we have… because God gave them to us!

7. There is a really cool verse in the Bible about God being our provider. 2 Corinthians 9:8 says, *And God will generously provide all you need. You will always have everything you need and plenty left over to share with others.* What do you think this verse means?

   a. God will always give you what you need.

   b. God is generous with us… which means He gives us lots of super awesome things.

   c. God will give us things and we're supposed to share with others what God has given to us.

8. Practice saying the first part of this verse together a few times: *And God will generously provide all you need.* – 2 Corinthians 9:8

9. What does it mean to be "PERFECT?"
   a. Never make mistakes
   b. Always do the right thing
   c. Never say something wrong

10. Do you know anyone who is perfect?
    a. No! Only God is perfect. All of us make mistakes, but God NEVER does. God is perfect!

11. How does it make you feel to know that God is perfect and will never let you down?
    a. Safe
    b. Happy
    c. Comforted

Polka Dot Girls ❧ Knowing God

week 2

4th and 5th Grade Group Discussion Questions

1. Tonight we learned about God and how there are three parts to Him. Do you remember what the three parts are?

   a. God the Father

   b. God the Son (Jesus)

   c. God the Holy Spirit

2. God the Father is our protector. What does the word "protector" mean?

   a. Someone that makes sure you are safe.

   b. The person that sticks up for you.

   d. Someone who fights for you.

3. How does is make you feel to know that God is watching over you?

   a. Safe

   b. Happy

   c. Peaceful

   d. Not afraid

   e. Confident

4. Part of God protecting you, is by telling you in the Bible some things that are bad for you that you should avoid. What are some of those things?

   a. Saying bad words or gossiping

   b. Being drunk on alcohol

   c. Not controlling the things you say

   d. Hurting other people

5. What happens when you don't follow God's protective instructions in the Bible?

   a. YOU get hurt because you open yourself up to the things that can hurt you.

   b. **Example:** If you don't control the things you say, you can say something that will hurt your friend's feelings and then they won't want to be your friend anymore. That will be a hard thing for you, so God tells you to be a good friend in the first place so you can avoid the pain of losing a friend because of the things you say.

6. God the Father is our provider. What does the word "provider" mean?

   a. Someone who makes sure you have all the things you need

   b. The person that gives you food and clothes

   c. Someone that gives you money

7. There is a difference between something you need and something you want. Name a few things that are things you NEED.

   a. Food

   b. Clothes

   c. House to live in

8. Now name a few things that are WANTS.

   a. Games

   b. Computers

   c. Clothes

   d. Cell Phone

It's important to remember that God promises to provide the things that we need. That doesn't mean that we get everything we WANT. BUT – sometimes God blesses us by giving us the things we NEED and some of the things we want. That is why we should be so thankful for the things we have… because God gave them to us!

Polka Dot Girls ❀ Knowing God

9. There is a really cool verse in the Bible about God being our provider. 2 Corinthians 9:8 says, *And God will generously provide all you need. You will always have everything you need and plenty left over to share with others.*

   What do you think this verse means?

   a. God will always give you what you need

   b. God is generous with us… which means He gives us lots of super awesome things.

   c. God will give us things and we're supposed to share with others what God has given to us.

10. Practice saying the first part of this verse together a few times: *And God will generously provide all you need.* – 2 Corinthians 9:8

11. What does it mean to be "PERFECT?"

    a. Never make mistakes

    b. Always do the right thing

    c. Never say something wrong

12. Do you know anyone who is perfect?

    a. No! Only God is perfect. All of us make mistakes, but God NEVER does. God is perfect!

13. How does it make you feel to know that God is perfect and will never let you down?

    a. Safe

    b. Happy

    c. Comforted

    d. Confident

week 2

"God is my Shield" Wall Hanging

Leaders: Make sure you do adequate preparation for the crafts in accordance to the age and skill level of your group. For younger children, have the shields cut out and the holes pre-punched. Older children should be able to cut out the shield, punch holes, thread ribbon and decorate in the allotted time.

Supplies Needed:
- Template of Shield
- Cardstock (white or colored)
- Scissors
- 3-Hole Punch
- Ribbon
- Crayons and markers
- Foam shapes, stickers, sparkles and pretty embellishments

Prep:
- Copy template onto white or favorite color cardstock
- Cut out the shield

What should we do?
1. Give each girl a shield printed on cardstock.
2. If the shield was not pre-cut, cut out the shield.
3. Punch holes around the shield.
3. Thread ribbon through the holes beginning from the top and ending at the top.
4. Leave enough ribbon at the beginning and the end to tie into a ribbon.
5. Decorate shield with crayons, markers and embellishments.
6. On the back of the shield write down the theme verse for this week.
7. Hang in your room!

Polka Dot Plus

week 2

Weekly Challenge

Grow – Grow your faith by reading the following Bible Story: **2 Corinthians 9:6-9**

Love – Show God's love this week by doing a simple act of service for a neighbor or friend outside your family.

Act – God is your heavenly Father. You are his child. God planned for you to be born. Talk to your mom and dad about the day you were born. In your journal, write down interesting facts about the day you were born. (date, time, place, weather) Then write down what you think you mean to Him? Thank God for planning you and giving you life! Next week, share with your group about the things you learned about the day you were born.

Memorize – Memorize the theme verse for this week.

*See how much our Father loves us,
for he calls us his children, and that is what we are!*

– 1 John 3:1

Parent Partner

One of the most important lessons you can give your daughter, is to give her an accurate view of God the Father. It's very easy for her to connect her image of our Heavenly Father with the earthly authorities in her life: her parents, grandparents, teachers, or other people of significance.

First of all, being loving and accepting of her is vital. Many children grow up thinking that they aren't good enough. Pour encouragement into her little heart every chance you get. Remind her that she is unique and special. Even when correcting her, make sure your instructions are constructive and loving.

And we all know that we are definitely "imperfect" authority figures. Be quick to apologize for moments when you react in anger or are impatient with her. And then be sure to remind her that although you are human and will make mistakes, GOD is perfect and will never fail her. Give her the foundation of His unshakable character and love for her to stand on.

GOD is perfect and will never fail

Polka Dot Girls ❀ Knowing God

week 2

Kindergarten and 1st Grade
Take Home Activity Sheet

God is the Best Father EVER! Below is the word FATHER. Match each letter of the word with the picture of the attribute the best describes what a great Father God is. Draw a line from the letter to the picture.

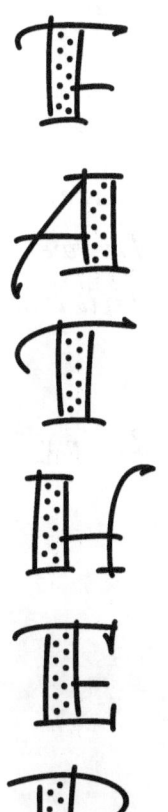

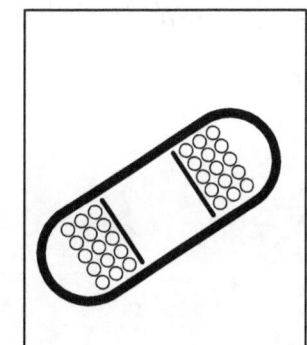

Word List

friend   everywhere   almighty
truth   rock   healer

47

In the verses below, write in the word FATHER in the blank spaces. All scripture NIV.

Psalm 2:7 – The Lord said to me, *You are my son. Today I have become your* _____.

Psalm 89:26 – *And he will call out to me, You are my* _____, *my God, and the Rock of my salvation.*

Isaiah 9:6 – *And He will be called: Wonderful Counselor, Mighty God, Everlasting* _____, *Prince of Peace.*

Matthew 5:16 – *In the same way, let your good deeds shine out for all to see, so that everyone will praise your heavenly* _____.

Romans 8:15-16 – *So you have not received a spirit that makes you fearful slaves. Instead, you received God's Spirit when he adopted you as his own children. Now we call him, 'Abba* _____'. *For His spirit joins with our spirit to affirm that we are God's children.*

2 Cor 6:18 – *And I will be your* _____, *and you will be my sons and daughters, says the Lord Almighty.*

Polka Dot Girls ❀ Knowing God

week 2

2nd and 3rd Grade Take Home Activity Sheet

God is the Best Father EVER! Below is the word FATHER. Write next to each letter an attribute from the word list that best describes what a great Father God is.

F _____

A _____

T _____

H _____

E _____

R _____

WORD LIST

friend   everywhere   almighty

truth   rock   healer

In the verses below, write in the word FATHER in the blank spaces. All scripture NIV.

Psalm 2:7 – The Lord said to me *You are my son. Today I have become your* _____.

Psalm 89:26 – And he will call out to me, *You are my* _____, *my God, and the Rock of my salvation.*

Isaiah 9:6 – *And He will be called: Wonderful Counselor, Mighty God, Everlasting* _____, *Prince of Peace.*

Matthew 5:16 – *In the same way, let your good deeds shine out for all to see, so that everyone will praise your heavenly* _____.

Romans 8:15-16 – *So you have not received a spirit that makes you fearful slaves. Instead, you received God's Spirit when he adopted you as his own children. Now we call him, 'Abba* _____.' *For His spirit joins with our spirit to affirm that we are God's children.*

2 Cor 6:18 – *And I will be your* _____, *and you will be my sons and daughters, says the Lord Almighty.*

week 2

4th and 5th Grade
Take Home Activity Sheet

God is the Best Father **EVER**! Next to each letter of the word **FATHER** write down an attribute that describes what a great **FATHER** God is.

F _____

A _____

T _____

H _____

E _____

R _____

Examples: Friend, Holy, etc.

Look up the verses below, write in the missing words in the blank spaces. All scripture NIV.

Psalm 2:7 – The Lord said to me, *You are my son. Today I have become your* _____.

Psalm 89:26 – *And he will call out to me, You are my* _____, *my God, and the* _____ *of my salvation.*

Isaiah 9:6 – *And He will be called: Wonderful* _____, *Mighty God, Everlasting* _____, *Prince of Peace.*

Matthew 5:16 – *In the same way, let your good* _____ *shine out for all to see, so that everyone will praise your heavenly* _____.

Romans 8:15-16 – *So you have not received a spirit that makes you fearful* _____. *Instead, you received God's Spirit when he adopted you as his own* _____. *Now we call him, 'Abba* _____.' *For His spirit joins with our spirit to affirm that we are God's children.*

2 Cor 6:18 – *And I will be your* _____, *and you will be my sons and* _____, *says the Lord Almighty.*

Polka Dot Girls ❦ Knowing God

Knowing God

week 3

God the Son (Jesus)

What's the Point?

JESUS CAME TO EARTH AND DIED ON THE CROSS TO GIVE US AN "ALL ACCESS" PASS TO GOD.

theme verse

"So now we can rejoice in our wonderful new relationship with God because our Lord Jesus Christ has made us friends of God."

Romans 5:11

related bible story

Sin Enters the World
Genesis 3

❋ Large Group Lesson ❋

Last week we learned about God as our Heavenly Father. There were three things we said about God the Father. Do you remember what they were?

1. He PROTECTS us
2. He PROVIDES for us
3. And He is PERFECT

Today we are going to talk about God the Son – which is Jesus.

Jesus is God's son. He was in heaven with the Father and the Holy Spirit, but there was a problem with people on the earth that God had created. How many of you have heard the story of Adam and Eve?

Adam and Eve were the first people that God ever created. Genesis 1 tells us God created man and gave them one rule. They were **NOT** to eat the fruit from a certain tree in the garden. But Adam and Eve did not follow the rules that God gave them, and the moment that they disobeyed God, **SIN** entered the world. Sin is not just the things that you and I do that are wrong – sin became a part of who we are. We are just imperfect people who have a part of us that is sinful.

> **Example:** How many of you have baby brothers or sisters? How many of you have watched your younger brothers and sisters say "**MINE**" and get kind of mean? How many of you have had your baby brothers or sisters hit you or be selfish? Now, my question is: Who taught them to be naughty? Did you teach your little sister to be mean? Did your mom and dad sit them down and tell them that they should scream and cry when they don't get their own way? **NO**! They were just born that way? And you and I were too.

Each and every one of us was born with a sinful nature. The Bible tells us this in Romans 3:23. It says, *"For everyone has sinned; we all fall short of God's glorious standard."* Every one of us makes mistakes, does the wrong thing, and thinks only about ourselves. It doesn't mean that we are bad – it just means that we are born imperfect. We are born with a sinful nature.

But **GOD** is **PERFECT**. He doesn't have a sinful nature like you and me. He never does the wrong thing. He has never sinned. He is perfect. And because He is perfect and holy, He cannot be around sin. He just can't.

God loved you **SO** much that He wanted to find a way to be close to you and me – even though our nature was sinful. And this is where Jesus comes in. John 3:16 says, *"For God so loved the world so much that He gave His one and only son, so that everyone who believes in Him will not perish but have eternal life."*

Polka Dot Girls ❀ Knowing God

week 3

Jesus is God's son. He is perfect and sinless just like God the Father. So God came up with a plan. Jesus would come down to earth as a person – just like you and me. He would be fully God and yet fully human. And He would live a perfect life… without sinning at all. Who knows how Jesus came to earth? What holiday do we celebrate when Jesus came down to earth? That's right – Christmas! Jesus came down to earth as a little baby born in a manger on Christmas!

WHO KNEW?

Another name that we sometimes use to talk about Jesus is Emmanuel.

It means "God is with Us."

Jesus came to earth for a very important reason. The only way that God could be close to you and me is if Jesus died on the cross and rose again. If He did that, then there would be a way for us to have a close relationship with God – even though we are sinful people. And so that is exactly what He did.

Jesus came to earth, grew up and became a man and lived a sinless life. And then when He was 33 years old, He died on the cross. But three days after He died, He rose again! And then He went back up into heaven to be with the Father once again.

When he did that, something amazing happened. Now we have a way to be close to God. Even though we are sinful people, because of what Jesus did on the cross, you and I now can have a relationship with God! Isn't that amazing!

There was a girl named Stacy who went to a concert of her absolutely favorite singer ever. She was crazy about this girl and could hardly wait to get to the show. After the show was over, she noticed people walking through a door that said "Backstage Access." She wondered what was back there and so she walked closer to get a better look. On the other side of the door, she saw the singer… HER singer standing backstage!!! Stacy could hardly believe what she was seeing!! She saw other people walking through the door, so she walked over, crazy excited that she was going to get the chance to meet her!

But the security guard at the door stopped her and said, "I'm sorry, but you can't go back there without one of these." He held up a lanyard that had a little card on the bottom that said "All Access." She was so disappointed. She knew that her absolute favorite, favorite, favorite singer was right behind that door and if she could just get through then she would be able to meet her and get to know her and spend time with her. But she couldn't get through that door without the "All Access" pass.

Then all of the sudden, a woman walked up beside her and smiled. She held up something in her hand. Stacy could hardly believe it… it was an ALL ACCESS PASS!!!! The nice woman looked at her and said, "Would you like to have this pass?"

Would she like to have this pass?!?!? Are you kidding me? Of COURSE she wanted the pass! Like CRAZY wanted the pass! With that pass she could spend time with the most amazingly awesome person in the universe!!!!!

She could hardly get the words out of her mouth. "YES! I would love to have the pass! Thank you so much!!" The woman placed the lanyard around her neck and Stacy walked through the door and got to meet her favorite singer.

And that is exactly what Jesus did for you and me. We were separated from God. We couldn't be close to Him because of our sinful nature. There was a big door between us and Him. But when Jesus came to earth and died on the cross, He made a way for you and me to have an "All Access" pass to God. We can have a relationship with Him. We can know Him. We can be close to Him. Through Jesus, we can be forgiven of all those sinful things we do!

Polka Dot Girls ❦ Knowing God

So – how do we get that All Access pass to God? We simply ask Jesus for it! We ask Him to come into our lives and forgive us for all the things we've done wrong and ask Jesus to come and live in our hearts. When we ask Jesus into our lives, He places a big "All Access" pass around our necks. We are forgiven of our sins and now can have a close, personal relationship with God. Romans 5:11 says, "*So now we can rejoice in our wonderful new relationship with God because our Lord Jesus Christ has made us friends of God.*"

The whole reason that Jesus came to earth and died for you and me was simply because He loved us SO very much. He wanted to be close to you so He provided a way. Aren't you so thankful that Jesus died on the cross for you?

Maybe some of you have never asked Jesus to come into your hearts and today you want to ask Him to forgive you of your sins and put a big "All Access" pass around your neck. Today you can invite Jesus into your life and begin living your life in a close, personal relationship with Him.

Would everyone please bow your heads and close your eyes? Jesus would LOVE to have a relationship with you. He died on the cross because He loved you so much and today you can ask Him to come into your heart. If you would like to do that today, please raise your hand and then we can pray together.

Closing prayer: Pray this prayer with me. "*Dear Jesus, I thank you that you came to earth and died on the cross. Please forgive me for all my sins and come into my life. I want to live for you, and I want to spend time getting to know you more so that I can be closer to you. Thank you for coming into my heart. Amen.*"

week 3

Kindergarten and 1st Grade Group Discussion Questions

1. Adam and Eve were the first two people that God created. What was the one thing that God told them they could not do?

    a. They could not eat from the tree in the middle of the garden (the tree of the knowledge of good and evil)

2. What did Adam and Eve do?

    a. They ate the fruit of the tree even though they weren't supposed to.

3. What happened when Adam and Eve disobeyed God?

    a. Sin entered the world and now we all have a sinful nature.

4. Have you ever done anything bad? Have you ever disobeyed your Mom or Dad or hurt someone? That shows us that we have are all born with a sinful nature!

5. Let's say this verse together a few times: *"There is no one who always does what is right, not even one."* – Romans 3:10 (New Century Version)

6. Because we are all sinful, there is a door between us and God. BUT – someone made a way for us to be able to walk through the door… who is that?

    a. Jesus!

7. How did Jesus make a way for us to have access to God the Father?

    a. By coming to earth, living a sinless life, dying on the cross and coming back to life again!

8. How can you and I get the All Access pass to God?

    a. By asking Jesus into our hearts!

9. Let's say this verse together: *"And Jesus answered, 'I am the way, and the truth, and the life. The only way to the Father is through me.'"* – John 14:6 NCV

Polka Dot Girls ❀ Knowing God

week 3

2nd and 3rd Grade Group Discussion Questions

1. Adam and Eve were the first two people that God created. What was the one thing that God told them they could not do?

    a. They could not eat from the tree in the middle of the garden (the tree of the knowledge of good and evil)

2. What did Adam and Eve do?

    a. They ate the fruit of the tree even though they weren't supposed to.

3. What happened when Adam and Eve disobeyed God?

    a. Sin entered the world and now we all have a sinful nature.

4. Have you ever done anything bad? Have you ever disobeyed your Mom or Dad or hurt someone? That shows us that we have are all born with a sinful nature!

5. Let's say this verse together a few times: *"There is no one who always does what is right, not even one."* Romans 3:10 (New Century Version)

6. Because we are all sinful, there is a door between us and God. BUT – someone made a way for us to be able to walk through the door... who is that?

    a. Jesus!

7. How did Jesus make a way for us to have access to God the Father?

    a. By coming to earth, living a sinless life, dying on the cross and coming back to life again!

8. How can you and I get the All Access pass to God?

    a. By asking Jesus into our hearts!

9. Let's say this verse together: *"And Jesus answered, 'I am the way, and the truth, and the life. The only way to the Father is through me.'"* – John 14:6 NCV

week 3

4th and 5th Grade Group Discussion Questions

1. Adam and Eve were the first two people that God created. What was the one thing that God told them they could not do?

    a. They could not eat from the tree in the middle of the garden (the tree of the knowledge of good and evil)

2. What did Adam and Eve do?

    a. They ate the fruit of the tree even though they weren't supposed to.

3. What happened when Adam and Eve disobeyed God?

    a. Sin entered the world and now we all have a sinful nature.

4. Have you ever done anything bad? Have you ever disobeyed your Mom or Dad or hurt someone? That shows us that we have are all born with a sinful nature!

5. Let's say this verse together a few times: *"There is no one who always does what is right, not even one."* – Romans 3:10 (New Century Version)

6. Because we are all sinful, there is a door between us and God. BUT – someone made a way for us to be able to walk through the door... who is that?

    a. Jesus!

7. How did Jesus make a way for us to have access to God the Father?

    a. By coming to earth, living a sinless life, dying on the cross and coming back to life again!

8. How can you and I get the All Access pass to God?

    a. By asking Jesus into our hearts!

9. Let's say this verse together: *"And Jesus answered, 'I am the way, and the truth, and the life. The only way to the Father is through me.'"* – John 14:6 NCV

Polka Dot Girls ❧ Knowing God

week 3

"All Access Pass" Lanyard

Leaders Notes: Make sure you do adequate preparation for the crafts in accordance to the age and skill level of your group. For younger girls, have the hole pre-punched as well as thread and tie the string prior to meeting. The older girls should be able to punch the hole, thread the string and decorate the pass in the allotted time.

Supplies Needed:

- 8.5 x 11" Colored Cardstock
- String or Ribbon
- Hole Punch
- Markers
- Stickers and Pretty Embellishments

Prep:

- Cut cardstock into four pieces
- Cut string or ribbon into lengths long enough to tie around each girl's neck with the lanyard.

What should we do?

Have the girls decorate the card with markers, stickers, etc. and write *All Access* on the card. Then have them write out (our cut out pre-printed verses) – with John 14:6 on it and glue it on the back of the *All Access* card. Punch a hole in the top of the lanyard. Thread string or ribbon and tie.

Polka Dot Plus

week 3

Weekly Challenge

Grow – GROW your faith by reading about Jesus dying on the cross and coming back to life in Matthew 27 and 28.

Love – Maybe you have a friend or a family member that doesn't know what Jesus did for them on the cross. Tell them about Jesus today!

Action – Take ACTION: If you have asked Jesus to come into your heart, tell somebody about it! If you haven't asked Jesus into your heart, pray some more about this really important decision and ask God to help you know Him better.

Memorize – MEMORIZE the theme verse for this week:

So now we can rejoice in our wonderful new relationship with God because our Lord Jesus Christ has made us friends of God.

– Romans 5:11

Parent Partner

This week we:

- Talked about our need for Jesus to make a way for us to have relationship with God.

- Discussed the fall of man in Genesis where Adam and Eve disobeyed God, and because of their sin, we are now all born with a sinful nature.

- Shared with the girls that each and every one of us are separated from God because He is sinless and perfect, and we are all sinful people. God wanted to have a relationship with us, and so He needed to make a way for us to be forgiven from our sins.

So He sent Jesus to the earth to live a sinless life, die on the cross, and then come back to life. His amazing sacrifice for us provided a way for us to be back in close relationship with God. Jesus' work on the cross provided us with a way to have "All Access" to God. We simply need to ask Jesus to come into our lives, forgive us for our sins, and we will be saved. Once we ask Jesus into our hearts, we are clean and forgiven and therefore can have a relationship with God!

We gave the girls the opportunity to ask Jesus into their hearts, and many of them responded! This is a great opportunity to ask your daughter about her relationship with Jesus and if she has asked Jesus into her life. This is the beginning of her personal relationship with God and it is really important that you continue to nurture and grow her faith.

In moments that she is apprehensive or upset, remind her that Jesus lives in her heart now, and so she is never, ever alone. When she doesn't know what to do in a situation, tell her that Jesus is very close to her, and will whisper to her heart how she should handle a problem. Reemphasize that now she has a personal connection with Jesus and she can talk to him anytime.

Romans 5:8 – *But God showed His great love for us by sending Christ to die for us while we were still sinners.*

Polka Dot Girls ❦ Knowing God

week 3

Kindergarten and 1st Grade Take Home Activity Sheet

Romans 5:12 says, *"When Adam sinned, sin entered the world."* Draw a picture of Adam in the garden eating the apple that God told him not to eat.

But Romans 5:8 says, *"But God showed His great love for us by sending Christ to die for us while we were still sinners."* Draw a picture of God sending Jesus to earth for us!

Polka Dot Girls ❀ Knowing God

week 3

2nd and 3rd Grade Take Home Activity Sheet

Romans 5:12 says, *"When Adam sinned, sin entered the world."* Draw a picture of Adam in the garden eating the apple that God told him not to eat.

But Romans 5:8 says, *"But God showed His great love for us by sending Christ to die for us while we were still sinners."* Draw a picture of God sending Jesus to earth for us!

Polka Dot Girls ✤ Knowing God

week 3

4th and 5th Grade
Take Home Activity Sheet

Romans 5 talks about how sin entered the world through the sin of Adam, and how Jesus coming provided a way for us to be forgiven of our sins. Read through Romans 5 in your Bible, and write out the following verses below.

Romans 5:12 _____
_____
_____

Romans 5:15 _____
_____
_____

Romans 5:16 _____
_____
_____

Romans 5:17 _____
_____
_____

Romans 5:18 _____
_____
_____

Polka Dot Girls ♣ Knowing God

Knowing God

week 4

God the Holy Spirit

What's the Point?

Jesus sent us the Holy Spirit to be our comforter, teacher, and guide.

theme verse

Then I will ask the Father to send you the Holy Spirit who will help you and always be with you.
John 14:16 (CEV)

related bible story

Acts 2:1-4

❀ Large Group Lesson ❀

How many of you have ever played TAG? You chase everyone around the room, and when you finally touch someone what do you say? You say, "Tag, you're it!"

Last week we talked about Jesus coming to earth and dying on the cross to make a way for us have an All Access pass to God. When Jesus came to earth, he picked twelve people called the disciples to be his friends and to travel around with him while He taught them all the things they needed to know about God.

But after Jesus rose from the dead, He told the disciples that He was going to leave. He was going back to heaven. John 16:5 says, *"But now I am going away to the One who sent me."* Can you imagine how the disciples must have felt?

How many of you have had a really good friend move away? Someone you really cared about who had helped you with a whole lot of things. When they told you they were leaving, how did you feel? You probably felt scared and worried and sad and lots of other things.

Well, the disciples felt exactly that way when Jesus told them that He was leaving earth and going back to heaven. But then Jesus told them something else really amazing. He said that He had to go away – but that He was going to send someone back to earth to be here with us forever. Do you know who that is? The Holy Spirit. Jesus had to leave, but when He left – he said "Tag, You're it!" to the Holy Spirit! Now it is the Holy Spirit's job to teach us and speak to us and show us all the things we need to know!

> John 15:26 says, "*I will send you the Spirit who comes from the Father and shows what is true. The Spirit will help you and will tell you about me.*" (CEV)

So Jesus went back up into heaven and a few days later the Holy Sprit came down to the disciples. Now, instead of Jesus teaching them all the things about God and helping them know what to do, the Holy Spirit would speak to them and guide them. And He is STILL here and will speak to you and me to help us know God better!

Now, the big difference is, the Holy Spirit doesn't have a human body like Jesus did. You can't see Him. You can't hear his voice with your ears like you can hear your teachers at school telling you things, but you can hear Him speak in your heart. Sometimes you will just have a feeling and that is the Holy Spirit whispering to you. We can't see Him with our eyes, but He is always with us.

OH, I GET IT!

In some ways God is like a family with father, mother, and child - three persons and one family. Just remember that the Trinity does not mean that we have three gods. There is one God with three persons.

Polka Dot Girls ❧ Knowing God

week 4

The Bible talks about a few things specifically that the Holy Spirit does.

First, the Holy Spirit is our:

➡ 1. Comforter

How many of you have a blankie or a favorite stuffed animal from when you were really little? It's the special thing that when you're scared or sad or tired you like to hold on to and it helps you not be sad anymore? That special blanket or stuffed animal brings you COMFORT. It makes you feel better whenever you are upset.

(**Teacher Note:** If you have an old blankie or teddy bear that you were attached to as a child [or you could use one that was or is your own child's] feel free to bring it to show to the girls as an object lesson)

And the Holy Spirit will bring you comfort too – just like your old blankie! 2 Corinthians 1:3-4 says, *"He is the compassionate Father and God of all comfort. He's the one who comforts us in all our trouble so that we can comfort other people who are in every kind of trouble."* (CEB)

Whenever you are scared or nervous or sad, the Holy Spirit will help you feel better. And you never have to leave Him at home like you have to do with your teddy bear. He is with you wherever you go, all the time! Say a prayer and ask Him to help you not to be upset and He will help you get through whatever it is you are facing.

The second thing Holy Spirit promises to be for you, is your:

➡ 2. Teacher

Sarah *Loves* her teacher, Mrs. Crenshaw. She is the BEST teacher ever. She shows Sarah how to do all kinds of really cool things and helps her understand stuff that is hard to get. She is patient and is always willing to listen whenever Sarah has a question. She is really encouraging and always tells Sarah she's doing a good job.

But she also helps her in another way. Whenever Sarah has a spelling test, she hands it in to Mrs. Crenshaw and the teacher takes out a big red marker and circles all the words that Sarah got wrong. When Sarah sees the big red marks, she knows what she needs to work on and the things she needs to try harder at.

The Holy Spirit is a great teacher. He will show you all kinds of things about God. He will help you understand the Bible. He will help you know what Jesus wants you to do and how to live a life that makes God the Father happy. John 14:26 says,

> *"The Companion, the Holy Spirit, whom the Father will send in my name, will teach you everything and will remind you of everything I told you."* (CEB)

But the Holy Spirit will also help you know when you've done something wrong. How many of you have ever made a mistake or done something wrong and all of the sudden you get a feeling in your heart where you feel really bad about what you did? That is the Holy Spirit! He will draw big red circles around the things in your life that you need to change and areas of your behavior or attitude that don't make God happy. He shows us these things so we can learn to do better and make the right choices.

And the last way the Holy Spirit will help you, is by being your:

➡ 3. Guide

Have you ever been lost? Have you ever looked around and realized you didn't know which way to go? Sometimes it's easy for us to get lost in our lives. We don't know what we should do. But the Holy Spirit promises to guide us!

Carrie had a big decision to make. She had been asked to join the traveling softball league for the summer, but if she joined the team, she knew that she would miss out on a lot of other activities she wanted to be a part of. She couldn't decide what to do! Her mom and dad told her that she could make the decision, but Carrie was torn. Although she loved playing softball, she was also interested in playing the piano and painting and even spending more time with her little sister. She needed help to know what to do.

week 4

So Carrie prayed. She asked God to help her know what to do. And one morning she woke up, and in her heart, she knew what her decision should be. It was so crazy! Nothing in particular happened, she just knew in her heart that she should pass on softball this year and spend time doing other things.

What changed? How did Carrie know what to do? Well, the Holy Spirit guided her into making the right decision. When she prayed, she was asking for His help, and so He gave her the answer she was looking for.

If you don't know what to do in a situation, why not stop and ask the Holy Spirit to guide you. Maybe you're not sure if you should say something. Ask the Holy Sprit if you should speak up or stay quiet. Maybe you're wondering if you should do something your friends are doing. The Holy Spirit will speak to you and help you know what the right thing is – AND He will give you the courage to do the right thing too!

Psalm 143:10 says, *"Teach me to do your will, for you are my God. May your gracious Spirit lead me forward on a firm footing."* God will guide you. The Holy Spirit will speak to you and help you know where to go, what to say, and how to act.

Aren't you glad that Jesus sent us the Holy Spirit! I'm so thankful that when Jesus left, He didn't leave us all on earth alone with no one to show what to do. I'm glad he "tagged" the Holy Spirit to come down to earth to be our comforter, our teacher, and our guide.

Closing Prayer: *Dear God, Thank you for sending the Holy Spirit to help me. Thank you that I can know that He will comfort me when I'm sad, that He will teach me things about you, and guide me into making the right choices in my life. Help me to know His voice. Amen.*

Polka Dot Girls ♣ Knowing God

week 4

Kindergarten and 1st Grade Group Discussion Questions

1. The Holy Spirit came to earth when Jesus left. Have you ever had a friend move away? How did you feel when your friend left? How do you think the disciples felt when Jesus left the earth.

    a. Sad

    b. Nervous

    c. Alone

2. Jesus told His disciples that He would not leave them alone – but that He would send someone to take His place on the earth. Who is that person?

    a. The Holy Spirit

3. Let's say this verse together a few times.

    Then I will ask the Father to send you the Holy Spirit who will help you and always be with you. – John 14:16 (CEV)

4. What does the word **COMFORTER** mean?

    a. A comforter is someone that helps us feel better

    b. Something or someone who helps us not be afraid or sad

5. What is something that **COMFORTS** you?

    a. Your mom or dad

    b. Pet

    c. Friend

    d. Toy

    e. Blanket/stuffed animal

6. How do you think the Holy Spirit can be our comforter?

    a. He is always with us so we don't have to be afraid or lonely

    b. He will help us calm down when we're upset

    c. He will remind us of God's promises to take care of us.

    d. He will give us peace when we're facing something scary or difficult.

7. The Holy Spirit is also our teacher. How does a teacher help you?

    a. They show you how to do things.

    b. They teach you about things that are new to you.

    c. They show you where you've made mistakes so you can fix them and learn how to do it right.

8. What are some of the things the Holy Spirit will teach you?

    a. He will teach you about Jesus.

    b. He will help you understand the Bible.

    c. He will help you know when you've done something wrong.

9. The Holy Spirit will also be our guide. Have you ever had a time when you didn't know what to do in a situation? Share your story with the group.

10. How will the Holy Spirit guide you?

    a. By helping you know what to do and what not to do.

    b. By helping you make the right choices.

week 4

2nd and 3rd Grade Group Discussion Questions

1. The Holy Spirit came to earth when Jesus left. Have you ever had a friend move away? How did you feel when your friend left? How do you think the disciples felt when Jesus left the earth.

   a. Sad
   b. Nervous
   c. Alone

2. Jesus told His disciples that He would not leave them alone – but that He would send someone to take His place on the earth. Who is that person?

   a. The Holy Spirit

3. Let's say this verse together a few times.

   Then I will ask the Father to send you the Holy Spirit who will help you and always be with you. – John 14:16 (CEV)

4. What does the word **COMFORTER** mean?

   a. A comforter is someone that helps us feel better.
   b. Something or someone who helps us not be afraid or sad.

5. What is something that **COMFORTS** you?

   a. Your mom or dad
   b. Pet
   c. Friend
   d. Blanket/stuffed animal

6. How do you think the Holy Spirit can be our comforter?

   a. He is always with us so we don't have to be afraid or lonely.

   b. He will help us calm down when we're upset.

   c. He will remind us of God's promises to take care of us.

   d. He will give us peace when we're facing something scary or difficult.

7. The Holy Spirit is also our teacher. How does a teacher help you?

   a. They show you how to do things.

   b. They teach you about things that are new to you.

   c. They show you where you've made mistakes so you can fix them and learn how to do it right.

8. What are some of the things the Holy Spirit will teach you?

   a. He will teach you about Jesus.

   b. He will help you understand the Bible.

   c. He will help you know when you've done something wrong.

9. The Holy Spirit will also be our guide. Have you ever had a time when you didn't know what to do in a situation? Share your story with the group.

10. How will the Holy Spirit guide you?

    a. By helping you know what to do and what not to do.

    b. By helping you make the right choices.

Polka Dot Girls ❦ Knowing God

week 4

4th and 5th Grade Group Discussion Questions

1. The Holy Spirit came to earth when Jesus left. Have you ever had a friend move away? How did you feel when your friend left? How do you think the disciples felt when Jesus left the earth.

    a. Sad
    b. Nervous
    c. Alone

2. Jesus told His disciples that He would not leave them alone – but that He would send someone to take His place on the earth. Who is that person?

    a. The Holy Spirit

3. Let's say this verse together a few times.

    Then I will ask the Father to send you the Holy Spirit who will help you and always be with you. – John 14:16 (CEV)

4. What does the word **COMFORTER** mean?

    a. A comforter is someone that helps us feel better.
    b. Something or someone who helps us not be afraid or sad.

5. What is something that **COMFORTS** you?

    a. Your mom or dad
    b. Pet
    c. Friend

6. How do you think the Holy Spirit can be our comforter?

    a. He is always with us so we don't have to be afraid or lonely.

    b. He will help us calm down when we're upset.

    c. He will remind us of God's promises to take care of us.

    d. He will give us peace when we're facing something scary or difficult.

7. The Holy Spirit is also our teacher. How does a teacher help you?

    a. They show you how to do things.

    b. They teach you about things that are new to you.

    c. They show you where you've made mistakes so you can fix them and learn how to do it right.

8. What are some of the things the Holy Spirit will teach you?

    a. He will teach you about Jesus.

    b. He will help you understand the Bible.

    c. He will help you know when you've done something wrong.

9. The Holy Spirit will also be our guide. Have you ever had a time when you didn't know what to do in a situation? Share your story with the group.

10. How will the Holy Spirit guide you?

    a. By helping you know what to do and what not to do.

    b. By helping you make the right choices.

11. What can we do to be sure that the Holy Spirit guides in our life?

    a. "Have our minds set" on what the Spirit desires.

    b. What does "have our minds set" mean?
        i. Set our mind to do what "we" want to do.
        ii. Or Set our mind to do what the "Holy Spirit" wants us to do.

week 4

Kool Comfort Pad!

Supplies Needed:

- Old or New White Tube Sock
- Fabric Markers
- Thin tipped permanent markers
- Rice (not instant rice)
- Ribbon
- Cardstock to pre-print the following instructions to go home with each girl.
  - Place the rice-filled sock in your microwave oven for 2 to 3 minutes on high power. Time may vary by microwave.
  - Remove the sock from the microwave and place where you need comfort.
  - The sock may be very hot. Protect your skin from burning by using a towel between your skin and the sock.

Prep:

- Cut a piece of ribbon for each girl.
- Pre-print the above instructions on cardstock.

What should we do?

- Decorate your white tube sock with your favorite color fabric markers. (Draw pictures and/or write today's verse on the sock)
- Fill the tube sock ¾ full with rice.
- Tie the top of the tube sock with pretty ribbon. Double knot the ribbon so the rice does not fall out of the sock.
- Warm in microwave and enjoy!

Polka Dot Girls ♣ Knowing God

Polka Dot Plus

week 4

Weekly Challenge

Grow – GROW your faith by reading about how Jesus sent the Holy Spirit to help comfort, teach and guide us in John 14:15-27.

Love – If someone in your family is feeling sad, lonely or afraid, give them your favorite blanket or stuffed toy and tell them about the Holy Spirit.

Act – Take ACTION: Pray to the Holy Spirit and ask Him for guidance when you have to make a choice or a decision. Be sure to try to listen for his voice. You can do it!

Memorize – MEMORIZE the theme verse for this week:

Then I will ask the Father to send you the Holy Spirit who will help you and always be with you.
– John 14:16 CEV

Parent Partner

This week we:

- Learned about the Holy Spirit.

- Discussed that when Jesus went back into heaven after the resurrection, He promised that He would not leave us alone on the earth, but that He would send the Holy Spirit to be with us.

The Holy Spirit's role in our lives is so very important. There are countless ways in which He speaks wisdom and discernment to our hearts, but today we focused on three main attributes of the Holy Spirit.

First off, the Holy Spirit is our comforter. When your daughter is sad, or scared, or lonely, remind her that the Holy Spirit is with her and has promised to bring her comfort. She can know that she is never alone, and that He will bring her peace.

We also explained that the Holy Spirit is our teacher. He will help us learn and understand the Bible. He will help us know God better. And He will help us know right from wrong. The Holy Spirit will speak to our hearts when we've done something that isn't pleasing to God so that we can stop our behavior and make the right choice.

And lastly, we learned that the Holy Spirit is our guide. He will help us make decisions and to choose the right path for our lives. Encourage your girls to pray about decisions and listen for the voice of the Holy Spirit in their lives giving them direction. Affirm that they CAN ask for direction and God will help them know what choices to make. The more independence they get, the more they will need to rely on the guidance of the Holy Spirit, and so nurturing and developing this part of their spiritual walk is so very important at a young age.

Polka Dot Girls ❖ Knowing God

week 4

Kindergarten and 1st Grade Take Home Activity Sheet

Solve the puzzle by substituting the numbers for the letters.

1	2	3	4	5	6	7	8	9	10	11	12	13	14	15
A	Q	I	P	F	V	X	N	Y	D	W	Z	K	S	G

16	17	18	19	20	21	22	23	24	25	26
O	U	R	C	E	M	H	T	L	J	B

__I__ __W I L L__ __A S K__ __T H E__

__F A T H E R__. __A N D__ __H E__

__W I L L__ __G I V E__ __Y O U__

__A N O T H E R__ __F R I E N D__

__T O__ __H E L P__ __Y O U__ __A N D__

__T O__ __B E__ __W I T H__ __Y O U__

__F O R E V E R__. __J O H N__ 14:16 NIV

Polka Dot Girls ♣ Knowing God

week 4

2nd and 3rd Grade
Take Home Activity Sheet

Look up each scripture in the Bible and fill in the blank. All scripture NIV.

But you will receive _____ when the Holy Spirit comes on you; and you will be my witnesses in Jerusalem, and in Judea and Samaria, and to the ends of the earth. – Acts 1:8

³Give _____ to the God and Father of our Lord Jesus Christ! He is the Father who gives tender love. All comfort comes from him. ⁴He _____ us in all our troubles. Now we can comfort others when they are in trouble. We ourselves have received comfort from God. – 2 Corinthians 1:3-4

I will send the _____ to you from the Father. He is the Spirit of truth, who comes out from the Father. When the Friend comes to _____ you, he will give witness about me. – John 15:26

I baptize you with water, but he will baptize you with the _____. – Mark 1:8

The angel answered, 'The Holy Spirit will come on you, and the _____ of the Most High will overshadow you. So the holy one to be born will be called the Son of God'. – Luke 1:35

Polka Dot Girls ❖ Knowing God

week 4

4th and 5th Grade Take Home Activity Sheet

Look up each scripture in the Bible and fill in the blank.

But you will receive _____ when the Holy Spirit comes on you; and you will be my witnesses in Jerusalem, and in Judea and Samaria, and to the ends of the earth. – Acts 1:8

³Give _____ to the God and Father of our Lord Jesus Christ! He is the Father who gives tender love. All comfort comes from him. ⁴He _____ us in all our troubles. Now we can comfort others when they are in trouble. We ourselves have received comfort from God. – 2 Corinthians 1:3-4

I will send the _____ to you from the Father. He is the Spirit of truth, who comes out from the Father. When the Friend comes to _____ you, he will give witness about me. – John 15:26

I baptize you with water, but he will baptize you with the _____. – Mark 1:8

The angel answered, 'The Holy Spirit will come on you, and the _____ of the Most High will overshadow you. So the holy one to be born will be called the Son of God'. – Luke 1:35

May the God of hope fill you with all _____ and _____ as you trust in him, so that you may overflow with hope by the power of the Holy Spirit. – Romans 15:13

But the _____ of the Spirit is love, joy, peace, forbearance, kindness, goodness, faithfulness, gentleness and self-control. Against such things there is no law. – Galatians 5:22, 23

You _____ me with your counsel. – Psalm 73:24

But the _____ , the Holy Spirit, whom the Father will send in my name, will _____ you all things and will remind you of everything I have said to you. – John 14:26

¹⁰ Just as Jesus was coming up out of the _____ , he saw heaven being torn open and the _____ descending on him like a dove. ¹¹ And a voice came from heaven: "You are my _____ , whom I love; with you I am well pleased. – Mark 1:10, 11

Polka Dot Girls ❧ Knowing God

week 5

Polka Dot Party

Polka Dot Party is a night for your girls to connect, invite their friends, and have FUN! Put together an exciting, special event for the girls to simply enjoy each other, do some fun activities, and tell their friends how FUN it is to be a Polka Dot girl! This is a great way to give the girls something exciting to look forward to and when they're excited about something – they tell their friends! Really encourage them to bring a friend from school or their neighborhood with them.

There is no "lesson" for this night, because we simply want the girls to connect. I promise you, if their friends have an amazing night – they will want to come back! This is a great way to introduce the girls in your community to your church and leaders. Make sure your event is AWESOME!

At the end of the evening, be sure to send guests a promotional piece about your ministry. This is a great way to invite them back for the weekend with their parents to church!

Polka Dot Party
Theme: PJ Party

Food: PJ Party Food

Games/Activities:

a. Hoola Hoop Contests by grade

b. Musical Chair! This is a great friendship building game. It is a version of Musical Chairs with a difference. Instead of removing a player and a chair from the game each time the music stops, only remove a chair! This eventually means that the group will end up having to squeeze onto one chair. Make sure the chairs you are using are sturdy because even the strongest chair will struggle under the weight of many girls!

c. Silent Interview (Similar to charades)
   1. Split the group up into pairs and have each pair tell each other three things about themselves - but without speaking.
   2. When they have had enough time trying to figure out what their partner was trying to convey, bring everyone back into the group and have each person introduce their partner, and the things they think they learned about them. This game can reveal interesting facts about each person and helps to build bonds between friends.

d. Tower of Mallow
   1. Give each small group several packets of both marshmallows and dry spaghetti.
   2. Tell them to build a marshmallow tower as high as they can.
   3. The tower has to be able to withstand its own weight, and the tallest wins a prize.

This game is perfect to teach girls all ages about teamwork, cooperation, friendship and coordination. It also helps foster new friendships among girls who haven't played together before.

week 5

Craft Ideas:

Option 1

K-3 or all grades: Decorate Friendship Pillow Case

<u>Supplies Needed:</u>
- Old Pillow Case
- Fabric Markers

<u>What do I do?</u>

Decorate your pillow case with markers...draw pictures, write special verses and sayings, have your friends sign their names on your pillow.

Option 2

4-5: No Sew Heart Pillow

<u>Supplies Needed:</u>
- Fleece (2 different colors)
- Scissors
- Ruler
- Chalk
- Pillow Filling

<u>What do I do?</u>

1. Cut two heart shapes from the fleece in the same size.
2. Cut the hearts 8 inches larger than the size of the finished pillow. (Recommended size 26 inches across and 22 inches long)
3. On one of the fleece hearts, use a ruler and chalk to draw a heart 4 inches from the edge of the fleece.
4. Stack the hearts on top of each other.
5. Use the chalk to draw lines one inch apart to make the fringe.
6. Cut the fringe.

    a. Start on the first chalk line and stopping at the center of the heart.

    b. Repeat until all the fringe is cut.

7. Tie the fringe.

   a. Begin at the bottom point of the heart and tie the top piece of fringe to the bottom piece by double-knotting them.

   b. Continue up the side of the pillow. At the dip at the top, knot together the top 4 fringes (2 pairs) into 1 double knot to cinch the opening more tightly. Then go back to knotting just 2 fringes until only 4 pairs are untied.

8. Stuff the heart with filling of your choice.
9. Tie the remaining fringes.
10. Wipe off any chalk that still shows.

Polka Dot Party
PJ PARTY

Polka Dot Party
PJ PARTY

Polka Dot Girls PJ Party!

Come for a fun night to hang out with the girls and do crafts, games, and have snacks! Wear your jammies and bring a friend!!

Where _____

When _____

Polka Dot Girls PJ Party!

Come for a fun night to hang out with the girls and do crafts, games, and have snacks! Wear your jammies and bring a friend!!

Where _____

When _____

www.ingramcontent.com/pod-product-compliance
Lightning Source LLC
Chambersburg PA
CBHW060516300426
44112CB00017B/2698